The World of
Swans

by Jennifer Coldrey

Photographs by
Oxford Scientific Films

Belitha Press

Contents

Note: The use of a capital letter for a swan's name means that it is a specific species of swan (such as Mute Swan). The use of a lower case, or small, letter for a swan's name means that it is a member of a larger group of swans.

Where swans live

Swans are water birds. They like open stretches of calm water (see left). You can find swans on ponds, lakes and slow-moving rivers. Many swans live in salt water, too.

The best kind of lake has lots of plants and small *aquatic* animals to eat. Plants also provide nesting material and shelter.

In the winter, many swans *migrate* to waters on the coast. There, the water may be choppy and cold, but it doesn't freeze over (see above).

The Mute Swan

Mute Swans are well-known in many parts of the world. They swim gracefully on lakes and rivers in our towns and in the country. Mute Swans sometimes make grunting and hissing noises, but they are usually silent. That is why they have their name, mute means silent.

Their original home is in parts of Europe and Asia. But now they also live in North America, Australia and South Africa.

The Mute Swan is a large bird with big wings. The beak is orange-red and has a black nail at the tip. The beak also has a black knob at the base, just near the nostrils.

Mute Swans have long, curved necks with thick feathers. They also have large black, webbed feet.

Other white swans

There are four other kinds of large white swan. All of them, like the Whooper Swan, live far north. Whooper Swans have straight necks and make a loud whooping call.

Bewick's Swans are like small Whooper Swans. Their call is a softer, more musical call.

▲

The Whistling Swan lives in Canada and North America. It has a high whistling call. Like the Whooper and Bewick's Swans, it migrates long distances for the winter.

The Trumpeter Swan is the largest of the swans. It has a deep trumpeting call. Trumpeter Swans are rare and live only in Alaska and northern Canada. They do not migrate south for the winter.

Swans from the south

Not all swans are white. These Black Swans live in Australia and New Zealand. Black Swans are about as big as Mute Swans. Each wing has a white band along the back edge. Otherwise, its *plumage* is black.

Black Swans live in very large groups – sometimes as many as 50,000 in one flock!

The Black-necked and Coscoroba Swans live in South America. The Black-necked Swan has pink legs and feet. Its call is weak and sounds like a toy trumpet!

The Coscoroba Swan also has pink legs and feet. It is small and has white plumage with black tips on the wings. It looks more like a goose than a swan. ▼

The swan's body

Swans have large boat-shaped bodies. Their streamlined shape helps them move easily through the water. They use their webbed feet like paddles to help push themselves through the water.

Swans use their long necks to find food underwater. Sometimes they tip their bodies forward. This is called 'upending'.

▼

A swan's feathers keep its body warm and dry.
Swans spend a lot of time cleaning and grooming.
They keep their feathers waterproof by smearing
them with oil from a special *gland* near the tail. The
swan rubs its beak on the gland and combs it
through each feather. This is called *preening*.

Once a year swans lose their feathers and grow a
new set. This is called *moulting*.

Movement on land and in the air

Swans are clumsy on land and can only waddle along slowly. However, their broad webbed feet do help them to walk on mud and ice.

But swans are very graceful when they fly. They have big, strong wings that make powerful wingbeats. Swans fly with their necks outstretched and with their legs tucked underneath. They use their tails to help them steer.

►

Swans are quite heavy, so they have trouble taking off and landing. When a swan comes in to land it pushes its big feet forward to help it stop.

Swans often fly together in a V or in a diagonal line. Some travel very long distances. They can also fly very fast – up to 80 kmph (50 mph) and up to 112 kmph (70 mph) with the wind behind them! In clear weather, they may fly as high as 1,500 metres. (almost 5,000 feet). When the weather is bad, they stay closer to the ground.

Migrating swans travel mainly at night. During the day, they stop to feed and rest.

Food and feeding

Swans eat mainly water plants. They use their flat
bill to scoop up food from the mud or water. Swans
sometimes eat small animals, too, such as insects,
tadpoles, snails and tiny fish. They often use their
long necks to find food at the bottom of a pond. ▶

Because they don't have teeth, swans swallow gritty
pieces of stone that help grind up their food. This
grit is stored in a special part of the stomach called
the *gizzard*.

▲

On each side of the swan's bill are little fringes.
These fringes catch bits of food and strain them out
from the mud and water.

Courtship and mating

Swans do not breed until they are three to four years old.

Male swans will fight to protect their *territory* when they find a mate. These two males are fighting to claim a territory. ▶

The male swan, called a *cob*, is bigger than the female, called a *pen*. Here, a male Mute Swan (on the right) ruffles up his neck feathers to show off to his mate.

▼

Before mating, the cob and pen go through a special courtship dance. They face each other and move their heads from side to side. Sometimes they rub their necks against each other, and dip their bodies into the water. Finally they mate, and the male *fertilizes* the eggs inside the female's body.

The male and female swans usually stay together for life once they have started a family.

Nesting and laying eggs

Swans nest in spring or early summer. They build
their nests close to water. A small island is a good
place to build a nest because it is surrounded by
water, away from land *predators*. Many swans come
back to nest in the same place year after year.

The cob usually chooses the spot. He helps the pen
to build the nest.

The pen lays one egg every other day until there is a *clutch* of five to eight eggs. She keeps them warm, or *incubates* them, by fluffing her feathers and sitting on the eggs.

The nest is very big, sometimes as much as 3-4 metres across and 1 metre deep! Its large size keeps the eggs safe above the water and away from enemies in the lake.

The cob stays nearby to help guard the nest and look after the pen.

The young swans

It takes five weeks for the eggs to hatch. The young swans, called *cygnets,* are born with their eyes open. When they dry off, they become tiny bundles of fluffy down.

The cygnets break out of the eggs with a special nail at the end of their beaks. This nail is very sharp and is called an egg-tooth. It drops off a few days after the cygnets hatch.

The young swans stay close to their mother for warmth and protection.

Some swans, like this Mute Swan, carry their babies on their backs.

Baby swans know how to swim as soon as they are hatched. When they are only a day or two old, they follow their parents into the water. Soon, they learn to find food for themselves. ▼

Growing up

As the cygnets get older, greyish brown feathers replace the down. The cygnets above are just over one month old. The Mute Swan cygnet on the right is about six months old. It still has a lot of greyish brown feathers and a grey bill.

The time when a young bird first flies is called *fledging*. Swans from the far north must be ready to fly south after a very short summer. They fledge in only two or three months. Other swans may take six months to fledge.

Swans are born in the summer and spend their first winter with their parents. Swans that migrate will have to go many days without food. They prepare for this by putting on lots of weight.

After their first winter, young swans usually leave their parents. Often the adults are eager to start a new family, and they drive the young swans away. Then, until they are ready to breed, the young swans stay together in large flocks.

Enemies and other dangers

Swans are large, strong birds. They will fight to defend themselves from attack. In fact, their hissing and snorting, flapping wings, and ruffled neck feathers are enough simply to scare away most enemies!

▶

This Mute Swan is angry. It has raised its wings and is moving quickly across the water to protect its nest.

▼

Adult swans have very few enemies. It is the young that suffer most. More than half of all cygnets die before the end of their first winter. Some die from cold, hunger and disease. Others are killed by predators.

The main enemies of swans are animals which eat their eggs and young. These animals include foxes, wolves, dogs, coyotes, otters and gulls. Sometimes large fish, like this pike, grab young cygnets swimming on the lake. ▼

Humans as enemies

Humans are among the worst enemies of swans. In the past, people hunted swans for food and collected their down for quilts and pillows. In the 19th century, the Mute Swan was killed off in some parts of Europe, and the Trumpeter Swan nearly became *extinct* in North America. Today, it is illegal to shoot swans, and special laws protect most swans in their *habitats*.

People also harm swans by destroying or disturbing their habitats. When water is *polluted* by oil, fuel, *pesticides* or other poisons, swans and other wildlife can be poisoned, too.

Fishermen can hurt swans by leaving fishing lines and hooks behind. Also, swans can get lead poisoning by swallowing the lead weights left by fishermen. The middle cygnet in the picture below is suffering from lead poisoning. You can tell because it cannot hold its neck up straight.

Friends and neighbours

Geese, ducks and other water birds often share a
lake with swans. In winter, large numbers of birds
may gather on the water.

Many water birds visit a lake to find food. Some,
like herons, will eat baby birds, and they can be a
threat to swans with young cygnets.

Swans usually attack only when they are threatened
by a dangerous enemy. But they will attack water
birds and other animals that come too close to their
territories and young.

Many water birds nest around the edges of a lake. The Great Crested Grebe (above), builds a nest like a floating platform. The nest is attached to reeds.

Other animals, such as otters, muskrats and beavers, may share the same lake with swans. This American Beaver lives in Canada and North America. It is a neighbour of both the Trumpeter and Whistling Swans.

▼

Life on the lake

Swans are mainly plant-eaters. Many other water birds feed on plants, too. But as this diagram shows, each kind of bird finds food in a different way. Some feed on different plants than others, and some feed in different parts of the lake. For example, when swans upend, they can feed in deeper water than geese. So, although there is competition for food, there is usually enough for all.

Competition for food

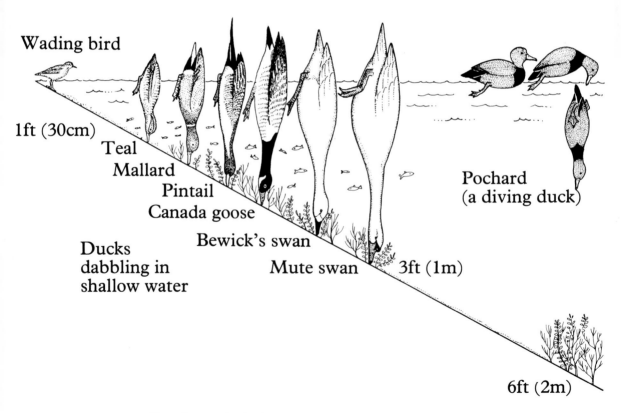

Depth at which different water birds find food.

The peaceful lake above makes a perfect home for swans. They need stretches of water where they can find food and shelter. Swans also need clean water and like to be left in peace. If we are to enjoy seeing these beautiful birds on our lakes, we must look after their homes, and protect the wild places where swans live.

Index and glossary

These new words about swans appear in the text on the pages shown after each definition. Each new word first appears in the text in *italics*, just as it appears here.

aquatic   living in water. **3**

clutch   a set of eggs. **19**

cob   a male swan. **16, 17, 18, 19**

cygnet   a young swan. **20, 22, 25, 27, 28**

extinct   no longer existing. **26**

fertilize(s)   to join a male sperm cell with a female's egg, so that a new individual can grow from the fertilized egg. **17**

fledging   taking the first flight. **22**

gizzard   part of a swan's stomach, with strong walls for grinding up food. **14**

gland   a part of the body which produces a special substance such as oil or sweat. **11**

habitat   the natural home of any plant or animal. **26, 27**

incubate(s)   to keep (eggs) warm so that they will hatch. **19**

migrate   move to a different area at different times of year, either to breed or to spend the winter. **3, 7, 13, 23**

moulting   shedding the feathers in order to replace them with new ones. **11**

pen   a female swan. **16, 17, 18, 19**

pesticides   poisonous chemicals used to kill pests, especially insects. **27**

plumage   the body covering (feathers) of a bird. **8**

pollution (polluted)   damage caused to the air, water and earth, from dirt, rubbish and poisons left by people. **27**

predators   animals that kill and eat other animals. **18, 25**

preening   cleaning and oiling the feathers with the bill. **11**

territory   piece of land or water which an animal defends against intruders. **16, 28**

First conceived, designed and produced by Belitha Press Ltd as *The Swan on the Lake*, with an original text copyright Oxford Scientific Films.

This edition first published in Great Britain in 1991 by
Belitha Press Ltd
31 Newington Green, London N16 9PU
Text © Belitha Press Ltd
ISBN 1 85561 085 X
Printed in the USA by Worzalla

British Library Cataloguing in Publication Data for this book is available from the British Library.

Photography: **Oxford Scientific Films Ltd.** for pp. 4, 5, 18, 24 and 31 (photographer G. I. Bernard); p. 22 and title page (photographer Alastair Shay); pp. 2, 12 and back cover (photographer David Cayless); pp. 3, 10, 15 *above*, 19, 25 *below*, 26, and 28 (photographer David Thompson); p. 6 *both* (photographer J. B. Blossom); pp. 7 *above* and 9 *below* (photographer Peter O'Toole); p. 7 *below* (photographer Margot Conte); p. 8 (photographer J. A. L. Cooke); p. 9 *above* (photographer H. W. Price); pp. 11, 14, 15 *below*, and 21 *below* (photographers David and Sue Cayless); p. 13 (photographer Barry Walker); pp. 16 and 21 *above* (photographer Mike Birkhead); p. 17 (photographer Martyn Chillmaid); pp. 20 and 23 (photographer Richard Packwood); pp. 25 *above* and 27 and front cover (photographer C. M. Perrins); p. 29 *above* (photographer D. J. Saunders); p. 29 *below* (photographer Harry Engels).

Line drawings: Lorna Turpin